We Are All Terminal, But This Exit is Mine

James Duncan

We Are All Terminal © 2017 by James H Duncan.

Cover art is an original painting provided by Alicia Frehulfer, who retains the copyright.

Book design: Bud Smith

Edited by: Devin Kelly

"Under the Bridge" originally appeared in Up The Staircase Quarterly; "Last Appointment of the Day" originally appeared in Kleft Jaw; "Strawberry Fields Forever" and "The Night No One Went Home" originally appeared in Unshod Quills.

Dedicated to my mother, Judy. Thank you for always looking out for us. And to my sister, Karla. Thank you for helping me remember.

7	There's This Dream I Have
9	That Gum You Like…
10	Day Beyond Day
11	I-90
12	The Green Carpet
14	The Line of Them Waiting
15	James and the Giant Peach
16	Trailer Trash
17	Virginia Slims
18	Burning October
20	What Were You For Halloween?
21	Food, Gas, Motel—Exit Now
23	All Those New Kids On The Block
24	Asleep in My Summer Grave
25	Last Appointment of the Day
26	Changeling
27	Don't Forget to Punch Holes in the Top
28	Mirage
30	Too Late
31	Beyond the Fence line
32	Oct. 31
34	Night Weather
35	Not Love But Better
36	Five Pocket Knives
38	Leather Shoes
39	Autumn Karma Awakening
41	The Night No One Went Home
42	Elliott Road, 1988
43	Exit 11
44	Absolution
45	Obituary
47	The Tundra
49	Instinct

50	The Cure for What Ails You
51	Long Before Twilight
53	What Lies In Wait
54	Spit-Shine Loser
56	Lampshade Wonderments
57	Ten Bloody Knuckles
58	Whistled While He Walked, Too
59	Strawberry Fields Forever
61	No Warning
62	Death is a Crack in a Mirror
63	Man and His Tools
65	We Are All Terminal, But This Exit is Mine
66	Large Green Trucks Will Come
67	Under the Bridge
68	Generation Nintendo
69	Tao of the Trailer Trash Kid
70	Native Songs
71	You'll Go Blind
72	Are You Experienced?
73	Jitterbug
74	Crows and Night Birds
75	Apocalypse Soon
77	Bones
78	The Best Laid Plans of Mice and Men
80	Wake Up Time
81	The Scary Parts
83	Phantom
84	Ghost Train
86	Dark Tunnel of Pine
87	Maladies & Memories
89	Hudson
90	My Gratitude
91	Hiding
92	Only In Dreams
93	One More Kiss 'Fore I Go

There's This Dream I Have

Outpatient treatment takes place in the children's ward, a hive of small rooms with curtains for doors, each with an IV stand next to a hard bed where, if I had arrived two hours earlier or later, I would have found a small bald child and his or her parents in number 27. Instead, I tell the nurse I'm fine when she checks on me and I lay back, stare up through the glass ceiling, my arm wrapped in foul-smelling purple gauze, and I slowly fall asleep again. It's the same dream as last week. I've had it three times since I began chemotherapy. That one time as a child when I walked the woods north of the trailer park alone, hoping to find the old tree fort Ricky's older brother said he built years ago. I missed it somehow and found myself in a clearing in the woods, quiet, a small headstone alone among the wildflowers and stunted saplings. It was sunny. I wanted to read the stone, read the date, but an overpowering sense of dread came over me, the feeling that I was intruding on something deeply private. I was eleven and lost and I didn't want to die alone. I ran from that place and it took me a long time to find my way back to the trailer park, only feeling safe again once I hit those streets, racing beneath those weak orange lamppost lights that had just clicked on in the evening dim. I never went back to that clearing, never asked about the headstone. When the nurse shook my shoulder she said everything was going to be okay, that this can be an emotional time for anyone. She gave me tissues to wipe my eyes and then pulled the curtain shut. My IV monitor beeped to tell me I had time left. I sat on the hard bed alone among a city of towers, streets never empty, the sun pouring in from above. I wanted to run but there wasn't anywhere left to go. So I waited as the poison dripped, dripped.

That Gum You Like...

We're happy in the back seat chewing zebra stripe gum from the corner pharmacy in town where mom buys the medicine that helps her headaches. Sparrows pinwheel in the Sunday morning light. I don't ever want to go to church again. I found it somewhere else.

Day Beyond Day

Dusty floorboards littered with flakes of scalp, skin, hair, human detritus in decline, medicinal wrappers, tissues, damp bath towels. The sound of a wounded animal escapes the throat, surprising the ears, the body shivering and losing. There is a memory of a car by the side of the road twenty years prior, a boy throwing up into the weeds and gravel by a shallow ditch, his mother coming around the car to rub his back. Just another trailer trash kid trying to hold it together until the doctor can prescribe some pink medicine that tastes chalky and sweet, and in this way the march to fifth grade goes on, sixth to seventh, more grades afterward, a whole life waiting beyond the sound of the car door closing. And now, deep breathing, no more grades, no more hand to rub the back, no sunshine glinting off the trickle of water in the ravine on the side of the road. Just a dusty floor and deep breathing, and maybe something beyond the sound of the bedside lamp clicking off for the night, but there's only one way to find out.

I-90

To this day I drive Interstate 90 and look for the painting I made in 3rd grade that flew out of my hands, out the window of the station wagon, swirling somewhere onto the grass shoulder. I like to think it's still out there, watercolor daydreams liquefied to earth and mineral infinity, waiting for the rest of me on that last exit day.

The Green Carpet

It was in a waiting room of chipped plastic tables full of wrinkled copies of *Highlights* magazine and cardboard flip-books about bears flying in hot air balloons, the scent of rubbing alcohol and Lysol. These children here are bald or soon will be and I run my hand through my own hair, find bloody fingertips, red robins in flight through my very flesh, flying away and away and away. Opening my eyes and counting my inhale/exhale, I see that the carpet here is lime green, shag, just like the green carpet where the small children of Green Meadow Elementary sat in the library, 1985, '86, '87...we read books about dinosaurs and planets and gigantic men who chopped trees in days gone by alongside blue oxen. There were books of women who flew planes and disappeared, and of ghosts who haunted castles, books of egghead professors with childish brain games, and books of children who had troubles just like the troubles we had at home or in our classrooms, on the bus, with bullies, siblings, nightmares, parents who disappeared, feelings of isolation, feelings. None of them had the troubles we had when we grew up though, or the troubles the bald children here have discovered. Publishers and sales reps probably don't like tallying such figures. Back then, Letter People lined the walls and a TV with Ramona played on rainy days. There were book club sales, book reports, and wooden chairs lined up along the wall, straight and small. All of us sitting on the green carpet. I believe the rain still falls on the windows there, while kids here grow old, fall down, their eyes drifting against the wash of a television glow in hospital rooms and daybeds, their blood and marrow melting, betraying, hounding them, the pages of their stories thinning out and fading blank. And then someone calls my name so I rise and walk across that green carpet to see how many pages my own story has left.

The Line of Them Waiting

Another fallen leaf. Yellow rice paper in the autumn infinity. We all rip and fold in predictable patterns. We never take that to heart. Seasons come with encroaching fire and the wind cries against the burn. Our bones lie russet red in this no-sun countryside. What comes next is well known—age a disease and youth the carrier. Roots bare from exposure and want. No dirt will cover these strategies. Like the line of oaks along the road leading home, the years bend in the wind of time, but only we break down, leaving russet red bones waiting for tomorrow, and tomorrow, and tomorrow.

JAMES AND THE GIANT PEACH

Window-glare sunshine streams through yellow foliage as giant worms and centipede shoes drown out the school-bus stereo. In my hands: a world within a world. A dream within a dream. None of us ever wake up, I'm told, and the sun is always shining.

Trailer Trash

Barefoot and whispering into the clouds above, asking the sun why high school boys in red cars drive by so fast yelling *trailer trash!* at me, standing scratch-legged in the crabgrass by the roadside dirt shoulder as horseflies bob in the heated hopes rising from my throbbing weeping only-a-child heart. Why do they say that? What does it mean? The sun burns silent answers down upon us all, a lawnmower dying in the distance, so little behind me, so little ahead, and all this fire in the sky. What will we do when it all turns to ash?

Virginia Slims

Billy lit his hair on fire trying to light one of his mother's menthols on the gas stove. Trailer park Sundays without supervision. A wonder any of us made it this far.

Burning October

We whispered that our secret fort would be this way, through the apple orchard and beyond the frog pond where a green metal shed lay deep in the woods at the end of a narrow dirt trail lined with ruts and ferns. There was room for a makeshift couch of logs inside and we ground out a fireplace and pounded a smoke hole in the roof of that metallic shed deep in the woods. A secret pact, a secret shake in that warm Autumn afternoon as we told ghost stories low and hushed and the trees radiant with the fire of our collective imagination. It was the best hue of life we'd ever live. We parted ways for dinner as night echoed across the wide horizon, and dinner waited hot and lush in this red-sky harvest season. But fate had other visions and cruelties hidden in the deep woods. Returning through the thicket we caught the first scent of smoke. Sirens wound through the oaks and elms and three of us peered from the hillock in the apple orchard and watched the firemen hose down the field behind our fort—the green car shed smoking and the hay field scabbed over crusted black. I never knew who returned with the matches that day, after we left for our nightly round of mother-made meals at home, but the smoke played through my dreams that night and many other nights that followed the death of our October fairytale. We never returned after that, to that shed in the woods behind the frog pond where that field lay mournful and dead. We'd lost something unnamable and sacred, and that place will remain forever haunted until my last Halloween tale is told. And let me say: there ain't many left to tell.

WHAT WERE YOU FOR HALLOWEEN?

Bear, space-man, dice, hobo, Robin Hood, scarecrow, pumpkin mask with a knife sticking out of the forehead, pirate, Darth Vader, ghost, others too, but I can't remember what. They ran too far beyond the neighborhood lights, so far now I can't recall, in search of candy...in search of joy...in search of...

Food, Gas, Motel—Exit Now

Tunnel-vision highway drive with numb hands and aching lead foot, I see the exit sign for home, followed by the sweeping curve of the ramp onto Route 9. There it is, just past the Hess station and the Knights Motor Inn, that old Burger King from decades past, right across the street from Green Meadow Elementary School, grades K-4, where I spent formative years on the library floor, in the music room, in an art smock, climbing a rope in the cavernous gym, where I received a giant green pumpkin for winning a footrace in October, 1989. I pull into the Burger King lot, the place we always stopped during field trips, usually afterward on the way home from bread factories, Indian trails, museums, stage plays and even an opera once. After waiting in line with great anticipation I'd always get one of two things: whopper with cheese with onion rings (never fries) and a brimming sparkling ice-filled Dr. Pepper, maybe root beer, or failing the whopper, the oval, that long chicken sandwich in an oblong shape. I'd pick up my order and go sit with friends, or alone, but always by the aquarium tank separating the restaurant proper from the sitting atrium and I'd watch the idle fish bump along the glass wall and eat my food and think about what I saw that day, enjoying the moment before we'd all pile back onto the bus to continue life and the little various hells waiting for us out there beyond the atrium window. Now that Burger King is closed, and I sat in the empty lot staring at the boarded up windows, shaky from the long drive, hollowed out from no food in eight or nine hours. Those boarded up windows hurt in a way I hadn't hurt in a long time, stupid really but it was a little like seeing the exit ramp for home turned over to grass and gone. Your parents' house demolished for scrap. No going back. Nothing to do but get older, hungrier, sicker, less willing to fight for what good things might be at the next exit ramp, the last exit ramp. But not all that weak just yet, not yet, still time left to pull out of the lot, wait to turn left at the stop light, and find that goddamn Taco Bell everyone else liked so much just a little further up the road.

All Those New Kids On The Block

My sister cried and screamed and said they were going to rule the world forever, those beautiful boys. My uncle laughed and said nobody would remember those *nancy pipsqueaks* in three years—"*Van Halen Rules!*" I guess they were both wrong. We all are, about most things. Except Cobain. I had a bad feeling even then that he knew something we didn't.

Asleep in My Summer Grave

Can Main Street survive without summer hopes of love? Without the glinting sheet-metal of ice cream stands at the ballpark where children daydream during pop-flies? Where have the endless afternoons gone? The late-night swims and the movies in the laps of grandfathers? The fields of dandelions rabid in the wind and scattered across the slopes of tender hillocks used for sledding in December? Too many still-frame memories, gorgeous and lost, fading through a deepening forest of age. Where are these children, my children, my hope for a chance to feel the pull of tire-swing gravity and sunlight once more? It's this cancer in my blood, killing them off one by one, year by year, name by name, and I carve each wonderment in stone and listen to the ghosts of this eternal summer cemetery, the cries and laughter somewhere out of sight, fading among the headstones, among the weedy graves of yesterday. So here in the shade of elm and willow, I make a promise that I will hold out for as long as it takes to make this right, to see that October Country again, that I'll wait for you and I'll wave as you come near, if you come near. I'll cross my heels, head in the grass, tombstone shade, my summer grave, and here I'll wait. This I promise.

Last Appointment of the Day

Across the table where picture books and children's magazines wait for small hands, across the fading carpet where plastic cars and wooden jigsaw puzzles lie scattered for playmates who may never return, there is a fish tank, the saddest looking pit of gloom ever, dark as a thunderhead in tornado alley, with listless fish waiting on death, floating nowhere in the murk. Elsewhere, there's a scream in my mind but there's no sound, a horror film on mute, internal and forever, and all these empty chairs surrounding me. Over and over again, all those empty chairs. The receptionist calls out my name. I get up and go inside while music plays from overhead and they shut the door behind me, at last.

CHANGELING

In my youth I became a werewolf, a changed thing as the seasons called for me. I turned pages and howled to the moon, ordered by the insatiable appetite within. I turn pages still, awaiting your command, hungry for more.

Don't Forget to Punch Holes in the Top

It was just a gravel lot when we crawled out of our mother's yellow station wagon and stood on the crunching bed of gray stone wondering just what she was getting us into. As Mom spoke to the land agent, Karla and I watched men in a big-rig truck back a trailer into a neighboring lot, as most other trailers on our street (soon to be) were also brand new, although none were to be as long as ours—a full 78 feet of American dream and blue-gray fiberglass siding. A home-owner, that's what Mom wanted to be ever since Karla and I could blink our eyes and cry out to the world, and now she was there talking to the land agent as grasshoppers jumped and flicked against my legs. Christ was there a lot of them out there in the middle of nowhere. That tree line, it was already calling me, and I saw hints of barbed wire and heard the tree frogs. I knew there was a pond back there. I could feel it in my bones. As the big rig drove away and the land agent got into his tan Buick, I asked my mother if Grandpa had any mason jars at his house that I could borrow. She said I could have the mayonnaise jar as soon as we were done with it. That sounded good enough to me as I watched the gravel lot fade from the back window of Mom's yellow station wagon. Life wanted life, contained if need be. Something to watch and something to monitor like tea leaves, like a canary in a mine. Grasshoppers by the hundreds never said a word, but I should have known.

Mirage

The playground was too old, they said, so they tore it all down and replaced it. It's much smaller now, compact, made of bright red and yellow plastic that deflects the morning rain. I remember when they built the first one about thirty years ago. Thirty years. I remember how that new playground made the newspapers and we all lined up and watched from the fence until they herded us back inside where we watched from the windows. Volunteers read to us or tried to get us to paint, to play 7-UP, anything as our parents, teachers, and hired contractors hammered away at the vast, unwieldy complex of wooden towers, tunnels, bridges, stairs, metal slides, tire-mesh walls, and everywhere gravel, little gray and white stones that, when walked across, sounded just like the sound cereal made in the morning when we chewed it fast to make the bus on time. It was beautiful. Now we had castles, we had battles, we had races to run and spaceships to fly, and they painted murals of monsters and aliens and dragons, glorious, glorious, everything we ever dreamed of. It was 1985, and it was the beginning of the best years of our lives but we didn't know it. All we saw was the playground out there being built by our mothers and fathers and teachers. We didn't see the college entrance exams going on at the high school down the street or the interviews at jobs, the insurance salesmen laughing in the backrooms as they slit open the stomachs of patients waiting for doctors who would never arrive. We didn't see the soldiers training for the war or the children blown to pieces in the war or the votes uncounted and burned or the cancer patients thinning out to ghosts or the policemen shooting the poor and insane or the night show hosts laughing into the camera or the politicians like red ants on honey devouring our parents one after the other. We didn't see the car breaking down on the highway or the people breaking down in bathrooms, we didn't see our grandparents dead, our parents dead, or any of the men and women who gave up, who just stopped doing anything about achieving everything they dreamed of as kids—they had no choice; they didn't make the leap. There was no ledge on the other side to grasp. But we still had dreams, being too young to know better. We still read of wonderful things in books and believed them, and we stared out the windows of our kindergarten classroom and waited for our parents to come and tell us it was okay to go home and go to bed to read and sleep and dream and then wake up to catch the bus, so it would all begin.

Too Late

Hey kid, don't build your late-summer hideaway in the poison sumac a week before you start fifth grade, okay? Not unless you want a rash all over your face, hands, chest, oh, oh god no, never mind I guess…

Beyond the Fence Line

It is one thing to be a child and believe all the world is waiting for you, that once you make it through fourth grade, middle school, whatever hurdles lie beyond, there is this *life* out there. It is another to find it, hollowed out, edges frayed, the tip of your shoes catching one hurdle, then the next, a domino effect of hell and memories coming up fast as you take the pavement face first, smash into the ground, cry out like a wounded animal, alone in the dark, silent. Looking back and seeing that kind of innocent wondering, it catches you right in the throat. What would your child self say if you could walk up to him or her playing in the old backyard, kneel down, and plead with them not to leave this place of bike riding and library trips. It isn't worth it. There's too much rain and fire, too much howling and heartache, a kaleidoscope of pitfalls. But that child self would know better. That child self would go beyond the fenceline, the barbed wire, beyond the corn fields out past the highway and keep going. There is no killing hope, even after the body quits and the mind turns to dust. You can look back and lament all you want. The child will go on without you.

Oct. 31

What a hell-cat evening, pitch-black perfect by 6 p.m. with the wind scattering every kid in the county down our street, door to door in costumes with bags of all kinds, scaring up candy like it was our job, our life's purpose. The white ephemeral clouds circled the moon like cobwebs in the stars. For the first few years it was just the trailer trash kids—my circle of friends and enemies—who would make the rounds, but sometime in the 1980s when the razor blades wound up in candy bars and those nondescript cherry red rape vans began to make the news, parents got the idea to drive their kids to safer neighborhoods to watch over them. Our trailer park out in the cozy middle of nowhere, out in the pine barrens beyond Nassau, was just the place for scared suburbanites to come and celebrate like the good pagans we all are deep at heart. We trailer trash kids didn't care because it added a sense of the unknown to our night, a flock of strangers to mingle with through the darkened yards and sidewalks, our feet darting in and out of flickering jack-o-lantern lights, the visceral scent of pumpkins and rotting leaves and makeup. Some trailers were set back in the woods or had shaded, dark pathways to their front porches, and a handful would play those *scary sound-effect* cassette tapes, which were so damn good that I'd sometimes sit under the windows and listen to those scary stories and sounds creaking through the speakers of a propped up boom box all night, imagining the walking dead, the howling wolves, the witches' cauldron. The build-up to that magic night was unmistakably heaven, the car rides to distant pumpkin patches and fall carnivals with hay mazes and cider donuts and dark wanderings around farm houses done up to look like something from a Charlie Brown special —my heaven. When that night finally came, the hours rushed by, life racing to oncoming death, each door a friend with a parting gift. The knowledge that the night was fading away hung over every joke between friends, every candy-trade, every costume change to go back out for Round Two to see if people would still give us candy at 10 p.m., and some did. May the gods bless their Halloween hearts. Each of their still-lit doors and glowing pumpkin skulls was a reprieve from the final moment when we'd admit it was over and walk home under those cobwebbed skies to wait through three more seasons for the only night that seemed to matter, for the only night that made sense.

Night Weather

When the winds come crashing down through the limbs and sway and rip the little leaves from their homes, I think of how it was for us, back then, lying in the dark during those wicked country thunderstorms at night, the fear of tornadoes in June, the worry of the gravel road leading to Nassau flooding out down by the abandoned summer camp. When the night weather comes now, I think of you and me, how it used to be. And a storm is coming. I can see it, feel it in my rotting bones. I see the silent flicker of energy in the night, far away but coming, rolling and boiling and simmering. My steps move quicker, but not directly towards home. Not yet. It is here in the throws of the night weather where it all can't quite reach me yet, the anticipation, the almost. If I can keep it here, it won't have me yet. But nobody has a grip that strong. Nobody can run that fast. There are other things with greater reach in this darkness. In this night weather.

Not Love, But Better

I never saw you again, but you were the nurse who held my head the first time the poison in the IV made me sick. You ran your fingers through my hair and held the tissues, told me it was okay, okay. I cry thinking about your voice. I hope someone, somewhere, right beside you, knows how lucky they are.

Five Pocket Knives

We were at war with that farmer's dog, a big fuck pitbull-looking machine that would trot the fence-line as our bus passed in the mornings. But this was summer and we had all day long to ourselves, free-range parenting gone to the extreme. Jason Wrigley had five pocket knives, one for each of us as we stalked the corn fields on patrol, a recon unit of not even pre-teen green berets. And then we saw it: the back end of that big fuck pitbull sticking out of a bush in our path, the only path back to civilization, 80 acres of empty farmland all around us, no one to hear us scream as it ripped us apart. The dog stood half in/half out of the bushes gnawing on something, probably some damn kid from the neighborhood, maybe even one we liked. Kirk started to cry silently. He was the dumb one but smart enough to know that crying aloud would doom us as we hid in the stalks of the corn field, single file in a line like snipers without guns, watching, whispering, wondering what to do but not knowing, each of us gripping our knives. I watched ants crawl in the clumps of dirt inches from my face as the heat poured down like syrup. On and on like that. Hours died among us as we watched that dog sit there half in/half out of the bushes until finally Jason says we have to bum-rush that thing all 5 at once if we're going to make it out alive. So we pull our shit together and huff ourselves into a rage, seeing in our minds the explosions and the blood and carnage and the grinding machine of death and then Jason is up and running down that trail like Rambo and we're off after him, screaming our dumbshit heads off, only to find a tree limb as thick around as a pitbull jutting out of the bushes. We laugh that one off and march home for the rest of summer, feeling a stupid glory drain out of us as the familiar rooftops came back into sight. Looking back on that now I realize that no matter the fight, no matter the enemy, none of us ever again felt like the heroes we were for those ten seconds in that corn field, bum rushing that damn dog, death and life in one brilliant flash blinding our eyes, throats, hearts. The universe knew greater secrets, but in that one moment, we had broken in and stolen them all.

Leather Shoes

The leather shoes in the flowerbed hid beneath low tulip bulbs and green shrubs dying in the sun. We saw them all the same, heels poking out, laces limp and frayed. As with torn pay stubs and voided checks, as with unused wrapping paper and empty beer cans in a ditch, the rotten death of a nameless man found face down in the Dorsey's back garden will go unremembered a decade from now. And someday so will you, and someday so will I, face down in our shoes in a little death-garden all our own.

Autumn Karma Awakening

Sanctuary: silent inside my room, thumbing through books and turning the closet, the bed, the square space beneath my desk into caves and pirate ships and haunted houses where the boy detectives in my favorite "Three Investigator" novels might roam, or the Disney characters from my illustrated encyclopedia set, hand-drawing them into notebooks by the hour, day after day. Of course, only after I finished piles of miserable homework. I'd give sullen replies and rejections to friends knocking on my door, people who couldn't possibly understand why a boy like me, all wiry thin and full of bike riding stamina and fevered mad-kid energy, would stay inside for months at a time, with winter coming no less (which would provide plenty of dull quiet times, so why not go out now when it was still nice?) but they didn't hear the little budding ponderous and quiet-wise Buddha voice in my head—and neither did I. Truly, we were too young to really know, and therefore it was the perfect time and age to be a quiet kid with a book and limitless imagination, scribbling worlds down on paper and teaching myself the meaning of going outward by going inward, without ever knowing a damn thing in the whole wide world at all. Then one day I went outside and smelled burning leaves and saw the yellows and reds in the trees, and I jumped on my bike and found the other kids and we fell in like I never went away, and sure they were happy, it was almost Halloween, which is my favorite, and in that way we all became Buddha-happy, simply because we felt the happiness inside stemming from the scent of autumn, stemming from the feel of bike pedals and leaves, stemming from some boundless nameless hope, stemming from being, just being. From being what, you ask? No one knows, and that's why it's true.

The Night No One Went Home

Potshots from the gristmill and away we go a'running. Weed stalks tough like tire irons thumping polecats skitter wild. In August, we dream of October. In October we dream of honor, and we know a ghost is waiting. Someone set fire to the gristmill the summer after the shooting. The coupe still sleeps burnt out amidst the wishing field of grain. The wind runs through that grain nightly; the moon watches with envy. Children think they are alive, especially when they play dead. Potshots strike the hollow oak where we once thought of honey bees and owl eyes in nighttime fevers; the moon a great dying tilt-a-whirl. With a match left in my pocket, I'll wait for you come, Autumn Moon, lest I burn it all down alone.

Elliott Road, 1988

Do you remember the yard at Elliott Road? The cherry tree stricken with some unknowable illness, not to mention the robins and spiders? Though we were still willing to climb the dying limbs, remember? Remember the pits in the lawn where our feet caught and tripped up as we raced around? We played so many thin-grassed games; bocce and baseball, tag and flashlight tag and red light green light, do you recall? And choosing the colors of cars? We learned orange and green were the colors Grandpa picked because he wanted to us to win. Blue and black and white were the real threat, the real game, and we'd watch and wait. Remember dancing on the hood of Mom's yellow station wagon? The smooth cool cement floor of the garage? The Christmas tree and the shocking clarity of the summer pool? Cold or not, we swam, do you remember? Where did it go? Where have we gone? Why does it hurt to think of the bay window waiting for us? To think of macaroni and cheese waiting for us, the pool table waiting for us. I cannot find that place. Somehow the roads all lead elsewhere, even when I try, even when my aim is true. Milestone markers of loss and lore send me sideways into strange neighborhoods, street signs felonious in their errant aid, leading me further away. I cannot find it, the way we used to be. Maybe it never was. Maybe this is all a fugue state dream. Or maybe this is just the prologue of a greater hell to come.

Exit 11

We all made fun of the trailer park right off Exit 11. What a dump. At least we had a basketball hoop and paved streets. Even trailer trash kids like us had a pecking order, and we knew our place—clipped wings but claws on our feet, and we knew how to fight for every inch we took.

ABSOLUTION

The nurse trailed after the little bald girl with an IV on a rolling metal stand and the girl sat and began drawing misshapen egg-people with fat markers that smelled of cherries and oranges and mint, which reminded me of first grade and homemade Christmas cards in December. The little bald girl with the IV drew a rainbow above her smiling egg-people and the nurse asked her what she was drawing. "When my friends come see me, they all look so sad, so I'm drawing them happy because I want them to be happy, even when I'm gone." Somewhere else in this universe someone is rushing his wife off to the hospital, someone is writing a letter and staring at it and throwing it away as they begin to sob, someone is walking down the street to buy half-and-half because their car broke down, somewhere parents stare through the living room window at their children building a snowman, and somewhere else lungs are crippled by cigarette smoke in lonely bedrooms at night, no radio, no hope, fuck it all. Somewhere there's a rainbow overhead too, drawn by a little girl in the grips of the insurmountable, smiling at all of us, absolving everything, all of it, whether we deserve it or not.

Obituary

I found a partial newspaper someone had left in the day room of the hospital ward where they stuck me with an IV. The only section left was the one that contained the obituaries, and as I read through and pondered the unique surnames of all the veterans and elderly folks that had died in the first week of October, I remembered what my uncle told me about the obituaries one evening while he babysat me, my sister, and our cousins. He lived in the trailer down the street and sat at the dinner table smoking his pipe, reading the newspaper, while the younger children watched Fraggle Rock. I wandered into the kitchen and he asked me if I ever read the newspaper. I said no, and he said I should. He showed me the obituary page, and I knew what it was, pictures of the dead, their names, their lives. He told me one day I would cherish those little boxes and lines as if they contained my very life, each word and period, each date, month, year, nothing left behind but ink and the steady hand of the newspaper editor to guide us home. Maybe he didn't say it quite that way—it was so long ago and I was so young—but I remember his solemn warmth and the weariness in his eyes, a sort of sadness behind a stoic exterior. I wanted to know so much of what he knew of this world, but he was wise enough to only hint at what would come. However he said it that night, he was right about the obits. We can delude ourselves about heaven and hell if we like, but fold the paper, sip your coffee, and never forget what the dead can teach the living through obituary ink, the smoke of their pipe, the fading words in the memories we keep.

The Tundra

We could bank on the power going out three or four times every single winter and that was if we were lucky. We were not lucky. When the power and the heat would go out, it stayed out for days at a time. There'd be no fridge to keep our food from spoiling, just the snow and ice outside on the porch. We could only heat one room, the living room, with the giant kerosene heater that looked like a brown, rusty R2-D2 droid. This contraption always terrified our mother, who would stay up all night to make sure it didn't tip over (couldn't tip it if we tried) and set the trailer on fire, killing us all like that one fire in the other trailer park down on Route 150 last autumn, so no one really slept, no one ever showered, no one felt warm again until the power came on. Being poor, we were used to reading, playing board games, or going out into the tundra alone to find out who else could no longer stand their families. Sometimes I would be the only one out there tromping through waist-deep snow, out past the wooden fence of the trailer park, the barbed wire, deep into the woods. I'd sit down against trees and imagine the world had ended, or that I was an Army ranger out on a lone mission—I'd wander like that for hours, trekking down creek beds, crossing streams and fences and almost hoping to come across a friend doing the same idiotic walkabout. I never did. They stayed inside their trailers until the power came back. But not me. Even when we did have power, I was always looking for a way out by reading a book or writing a story or just creating a fictional life in my head, or going out into the woods alone. I was always the escape artist, aching for some fantastical life away from the trailer park, the island of homes surrounded by miles of woods, farms, and what seemed like illimitable nothingness. To this day the mental games I played, the fake lives I created—I still do that, at work, at home, married, single, dating, sitting in waiting rooms, sitting with an IV dripping poison in my arm, slowly slipping my head beneath the water, I am always ready for my way out, ready for my escape—still wading through waist-deep snow, alone on the tundra forever.

INSTINCT

His eyes always watered in cold weather. It looked like he was crying but he wasn't, and the only time he did cry was when he caught my surprise right jab square in his face for making fun of my last name one too many times. I still think of it now and then, the feeling of socking Jason in the mouth, hardly any damage, just surprise, tears streaming down on instinct. He came after me the next day at the bus stop and told me my "ass was grass" if I ever did that again. I reminded him it was November, so he'd have to wait an awful long time to see any grass; which didn't make much damn sense and even when I shouted it at his back it felt weak and stupid. He sneered back at me as geese flew overhead in their V-formation, late for the sun, but getting there. We never spoke of that, or of anything, ever again.

THE CURE FOR WHAT AILS YOU

The small white pills (2) you eat whole will choke the cancer down in your cells. The other white pills (2) keep your stomach from wrenching out of its moorings and melting away. The green and white capsules stave off infection but make your skin burn in the light of the sun. So do the blue ones. So do the massive white horse tablets you choke down with a pint of water per pill. The gray cloth-covered hardback is the one filled with ghost stories. The thin white hardcovers are the Disney encyclopedias you read when you want to imagine life beyond the walls. The multicolored paperbacks are the Chronicles of Prydain, and you shiver at the thought of the Cauldron-born seeking you out with dead eyes. The tattered thin hardcover with the blue cloth spine is Steinbeck, and he will force the illness from your chest and make you cry and leave you well again, if only for an hour. The pink liquid is for your stomach, and Mom doles it out with a thick plastic spoon and it tastes like strawberry chalk and will remain within you forever. The clock in the corner is ticking the minutes, round plastic Mickey in your youth, classic black and white at post-diagnosis 30, and you keep hanging on for a grandfather clock, taking life one dose at a time, ticking, swallowing, turning the page, desperate for more pain, eager for more nausea, because it means you're still here, still moving, heading somewhere, anywhere but death.

Long Before Twilight

There were ghosts everywhere; I borrowed book after book from the library saying so, amazed and stunned that they kept this knowledge out in the open and available for anyone to read. I read about real life haunted forests and abandoned houses (like so many I knew from my own treks through the woods) and I read about witches, and then werewolves. The werewolf book was the one that stayed with me the longest, its tattered cloth binding faded and tearing, pulled from the deepest shelf of the elementary school library where no conservative school board ethics task force committee would find it. Inside there were ancient descriptions of how to turn yourself into a werewolf, complete with gibberish incantations and lists of roots and animal innards to collect. I often wondered, do I dare go into the wheat fields at night (where I knew the coyotes roamed with their red eyes) and try? Did I dare? Did I wish for that curse? I often wondered these things during October bus rides home from school or rides home from an evening visit with our grandparents, but it never happened. I never worked up the courage to damn myself at the mere age of nine, and to this day I think back and smile about that silly book, even looked for it on the internet once but couldn't find it. When I walk home from the bars now or from a late night in the office, I sometimes look up at the full moon and think about being nine years old riding the school bus and reading that book, and even standing on the edge of the wheat fields beyond the trailer park fence at dusk, looking out at all of those coyote packs with their nimble red eyes blinking back at me, wondering which fate would be worse. But of course, they all lead to the same road, the same exit, the same howling end.

What Lies In Wait

When you walk the cornrows of August alone, you pause, you know a silence that will follow you into every empty waiting room for the rest of your life. Rustling ears of green, step ahead, continue into the sun, into the coming harvest, and listen for your name.

Spit-Shine Loser

Bill Tomlison was a jock-type high-school kid who lived down the street, and he was big enough and generally cool enough that most of us considered him more of an adult than what we were (just kids). One afternoon close to the end of the school year I was walking down the street dribbling my basketball heading down to the hoop, and I saw him in a tuxedo. He was getting into his beat-up T-bird looking real sharp with his mullet and black duds, his shoes all spit-polished and shining. I asked him where he was going so dressed up, me being unaware of school dances and dating at that age. That's exactly where he was going, to pick up a beautiful woman named Danielle Maricotta and then going to the high school dance. He had a gleam in his eye I hadn't seen in anyone's eyes before, a real magic that set me unbalanced for half-a-second. I wondered about this beautiful woman as he climbed in and revved his car out of the driveway and drove away beyond the pine trees and the farmer's fields toward town, off to pick up Danielle Maricotta. A week later I saw him sitting on his bumper in dirty jeans with his hands all oily from working on his T-bird. I stopped and asked him about the dance, wanting to hear him say the name "Danielle Maricotta" again, but he just picked up a rag to wipe his hands, spat at the ground, and said, "Kid, you'll never get a first-class woman with a third-class soul, and that's all we have around here." He turned away then, and I didn't know him well enough to ask him what the hell he meant, but

I thought about what he said for a long time, sitting in bed in the dark wondering if I'd ever get to wear a tuxedo and dance with a beautiful woman, or if Bill Tomlison's evening in his spit-shined shoes was as close as any of us would get.

Lampshade Wonderments

Establish what grip? At night when there is nothing to hold, what grip? What hand is holding what invisible solace? All the world disappears when you jump ship into the everything-nothing Void of eternal sleep, an alternate life like a skipping record, the needle returning to wax as you close your eyes and nothing of the day-life remains. No needles into arms remain, no insurance claims overdue, no ER waiting rooms at 11 pm on a Friday because the blood won't stop pouring out of your stomach. In this waking world you cannot dig a foothold when the digging dies at dusk, can't grasp a moth when the wings blow away like dust. You have to let it go, and live again when you're most dead to the world. How can one maintain such a polar-life? Where are the poles? There are none, your child self knew that somehow, there's simply a center rolling around and around—one ever birthing dying lifetime sun sending signals through the Void. Within this moonlit story your soul whispers from years beyond, years ago, telling you secrets as you turn off the bedside lamp and embrace the darkness within the dark, wonderments eternal at last.

Ten Bloody Knuckles

I picked up my backpack and climbed aboard the bus, sitting quietly among the deafening buzz of gaping, chattering onlookers. Those who saw the fight that bloodied my knuckles down at the bus stop couldn't rat me out to the driver fast enough, and my poor sister sat ashamed in the front as I buried myself in the very last seat. The driver started back to school and radioed in my misconduct, and not only was this to go on my "permanent record," but I had lost my privileges as as "Bus Buddy" forever, a Bus Buddy being a title given to 4th graders who are allowed to "help" drivers by telling other kids to be quiet and behave on the bus ride home, which was a shit job anyway, and I didn't give a damn what they did with their titles and their fictional permanent records. All I ever did was sit in the back and read by myself anyway, trying to ignore the mobs of ugly, leering, hee-haw trailer trash kids all around me (of which I was one and would forever be one) and that's all I'd do from then on too—that and use my newfound dissonance to inject anyone who looked my way with the idea that maybe they shouldn't fuck with the bookworm any more.

Whistled While He Walked, Too

Billy Boot, they called him, some loner who lived up the hill. He walked into the village across the farmers' fields a few days a week using the side of the county road, probably a ninety minute walk each way. He'd pass the trailer park entrance and the church at the corner down yonder, the cemetery beyond, fields of wheat and corn, pine trees thick with darkness and mystery, and eventually into the edge of town, past the fish fry stand and the pharmacy, into the only diner that was open for breakfast, lunch, *and* dinner. It was June when the first kid went missing, and October when the second kid left the corner bus stop and wasn't seen again, and those boots Billy wore sure would gleam in the sunshine, gleam long into that Indian summer. That day finally came when one of the O'Leary twins ran through the park screaming, couldn't even speak straight over the tears, but we all knew what the finger pointing up the long hill leading out into the outer boondocks meant. A whole bunch of us ran to the edge of the road and watched as county sheriff cruisers whipped by, some staties too, and Patrick's mother heard the news from a phone call—they found Billy up there, swinging from a barn rafter mere inches off the ground, his black leathers all polished and gleaming with a pile of little school shoes in the corner, cleaned up, almost like new, but not quite.

Strawberry Fields Forever

The strawberry fields grew on all sides of the colonial-era brick farmhouse, right up to the edge of the wraparound. It was a stout red home built by the hands of strawberry farmers and now maintained by an elderly strawberry farmer and his wife, who stared down from the second story window of that brick house at all hours. They lived with the farmer's grown son, who walked around with some uncertain handicap of the body and mind, always present, aiming to help. I picked as fast as I could when the farmer or his slower son spoke to my mother or to other nearby pickers or when the old woman stared down from her window tower watching us. But when they were all gone I ate berries fresh from the dirt. No one needed to wash those berries. They were stymied with bugs often enough, and were small, but they were real and they were raw and juicy in the summer sun. I recall the sweat of that sun falling down on us as we picked up our full baskets (my stomach also full) and walked to the wraparound porch of the brick house. The farmer's son always wore overalls, blue jean overalls with dirt scuffed around his knees and ankles, and he'd talk kind and steady to my mother in a purposeful cadence, as if he were reciting to a class of students who might mock him, but we never mocked him. I knew he was just a strawberry farmer's son, a noble thing if an unthought of thing, and even as a child I realized that being one was better than being like most other men I saw in the world —with or without the handicap. Sometimes the old farmer would say goodbye as we prepared to leave, sitting on his porch, tired and talkative and older than any man I had ever seen in my life. They'd take our few dollars and we would walk back to our car, load the car, drive away. Maybe we'd be back later that month, or that summer, sometimes we never went at all. Many of those summers went by, the absent summers, and I am glad I have not been back since the age of eleven or twelve. I don't want to see how the old woman no longer watches from her window tower. Or how the old man no longer sits on his porch in the sunlight. I don't want to see how the farmer's grown son dealt with the banks or the funeral homes or the land investors or the neighbors or the nurses at the hospital or the whole world crashing down on him. I want to close my eyes and look up from the dirt, the rows of fire engine red strawberries, and see them there, all of them, and see my mother there picking beside me, putting each strawberry into a yellow bowl. I want to put one more strawberry in my mouth and never open my eyes again. That would be a fine summer day indeed.

No Warning

We could tell a storm was on the way by the whites of the leaves swirling upward in an ocean swell, a foliage sea giving away secrets, the treetops swaying a violent dance. These storms were rare, the hungry kind. Kids raced home on bikes all around but I waited, I watched. The whites and towels on the clothesline whipped like signal flags on a ship at sea as my mother reeled them in, throwing them into a basket, calling out for us to get inside. The clouds were black now. It was coming. The forest reached for us. Cold currents cut through the wind and whichever way I looked I saw the remaining children and trailer park residents running for shelter, doors closing, mothers chasing in cats or winding up car windows. Tornado season in upstate New York, high June, annual panic, rose gold skies turning catatonic black. I stood in the grass and let that wind crawl over me, faster and colder, feeling the moisture in the air, the rain coming, hail coming, hell coming, thunderheads so low I could climb up inside and never come back. It was upon us, the thick pummel of rain, just a drop or two at first, holding back. I never ran home. I wanted to know. I wanted it to melt me down and sweep me away into the night. Little did I know it would, in good time, a storm all my own rushing across the corn fields and pine barrens, a darkness within the dark, with no warning at all.

Death is a Crack in a Mirror

Death is a crack in a mirror that widens slowly over time and shows the black chipped underlaying beneath the silver reflection and it grows, and grows, every morning a little more void, and it watches you watch yourself until you aren't there to see it some dismal, rainy morning—complete.

Man and His Tools

The bullfrogs were enormous, at least the size of softballs, and there were enough there to keep us busy all summer. They were crafty, always leaping at the right moment. The two or three times a year when you'd actually catch one you were a true champion. I mean, the kids would talk about you all week, and no one needed pictures to prove anything, they believed you when you said you caught and released the biggest bullfrog on record. There was honor in the hunt. Until someone dashed a frog with a rock and somehow that caught on —catch and kill for sport and laughs. The kids at the south end of the park came around more often with their sticks and bats and nets to make it easier. You could see something new in the faces of the kids around the neighborhood. A dead joy frothing in the whites of their eyes. After a couple summers of that, there wasn't much reason to go back to the frog pond anymore. It was just a scummy pond now. An empty swamp. But whenever spring turned to summer I still thought of the frogs and I'd sometimes go and sit on the little hill beside the eastern edge of the pond and I'd wait and listen and hope that one frog would appear and hold out against the human tide. Even now when I ride the subways to go to work or to the hospital here in the city, where frog ponds are just a dream, I sometimes think back to sitting on that hill and waiting, wondering: who holds the rock that will take my lungs, destroy my heart, end my life? I close my eyes and open my eyes and I see the tools of man.

We pull into the next stop on the Q and I tighten my grip to hold on as long as I can.

WE ARE ALL TERMINAL, BUT THIS EXIT IS MINE

There is a cancerous foliage blooming in my flesh, my blood, skin, eventually organs, bones. My reflection in the car window shows no signs of the scythe and it may be years yet, but the years come for everyone: memories first, the blood later, the breath at last. It is a blurred doppelgänger in the car window, healthy looking, if distorted from the rain, a steady rain pecking at the glass, blurring the view of the street where I used to ride bikes and scooters, used to trick-or-treat, rain pelting the rooftop of my former home and the leaves of the squat oak outside my window where we'd play soldier, lay in the grass and stare at the stars, and like the rain falling on that old trailer, peck by peck, life is eaten away, peck by peck, from inside out, rampant white blood cells like blizzard snowflakes falling on a tundra, building up, suffocating life, leaving behind a rictus corpse ravaged, preserved, maybe even still able to drive, if one gives the foot a push down on the pedal, veering away from the past, aiming for the future, the country lane, the highway, the exit ramp, the final exit ramp, and soon no car needed, climbing out, closing the door, one foot before the other, with a heavy hand resting on my shoulder guiding the way through the dark.

LARGE GREEN TRUCKS WILL COME

We stacked dead and dying tree branches along the edge of the road, gnarled arms, thick and useless foliage, cast aside to make the world easier for others, and the large green trucks will come next week and take them away. Old men heap on clippings from a thousand rose bushes, from nameless shrubs and weeds, from gardens and from willow trees. The plumber down the block makes a scrap wood pyre, adding stripped fencing, leaving the nails to gouge the nearing sky. An old typewriter is placed beside a box of corn husks and hay bales, rotten and feral. A refrigerator appears and people think of suffocation and their children and small pets. More limbs. More leaves and grass shavings. More junkyard ornaments. More people, falling all the time into the piles, digging, casting, coming, going, their lives, their hatred, their time, their love for their own thoughts piled high, piled to the sky, waiting for the green trucks to come. There's a box that says "FREE" but no one takes that shit. Not even the green trucks will come for it. Some things will never be another man or woman's treasure—every trailer trash kid knows this too soon.

Under the Bridge

If Anthony Keidis could have kept his shirt on, Bennie's step-dad might not have hated the idea of MTV so much when he caught us lazing about in the summertime watching music videos instead of *starting a baseball game with the other boys* or whatever shit he was hollering as he slapped off the Red Hot Chili Peppers and kicked us out through the screen door hanging desperate and crying against its hinges, soon to burn down like the rest of Bennie's house later that autumn, but it was still our summer of indolent discontent, and we wandered around the streets and alleyways of the trailer park wondering what it would take to start a band, settling on the idea of just finding someone who was home alone with no parents so we could watch MTV again and hope for Nirvana or maybe Pearl Jam's "Jeremy," a video that scared the hell out of both of us 'cause we each knew a creepo in our respective grades who might snap one day. But that was one day in the future, it was still our summer now, damned hot, full of all kinds of futures. All we wanted was a little lazy rebellion before dinner, and that's about all we got too.

Generation Nintendo

So this is addiction, renegade children willing to carve their days and nights away breathless for the 8-bit paradise. That music they play in Zelda, Link fighting off the hordes, that herky way I jumped when Mario jumped, how I ruined family gatherings by slipping away to go play Excitebike, infuriated when they pulled the plug. And Double Dragon, holy shit! Can I spin-kick like that in real life? I'll have to try tomorrow. Master Blaster, Gauntlet, Paperboy. How are these even beatable? Reset button confidence got me through such insomniac delights, but there'd be no Game Genie for what waited out beyond the pines. No Tanooki Suit. But even facing the hell of employment or unemployment or watching midnight election numbers roll in that would doom your entire generation, or of watching an ex-wife slam the trunk shut and drive the last of her things away to go love the man she'd been loving all along, a part of me felt like that music in Zelda would never become obsolete. It would always shine with a force to see one day turn into the next. Fuck the pain and the horror. Blow into that cartridge and light this fucking world up, cackling all the while like that Duck Hunt dog, firing away until they come to pull the plug for good.

TAO OF THE TRAILER TRASH KID

The thing about growing up in a trailer park, for me at least, was that I didn't fit in anywhere. In the park I was too bookish, too quiet, the nerd who didn't like the drag races two towns over on Wednesdays and who dressed up for Halloween maybe two years too long. At school, I was just another trailer trash kid who took "that" bus route with all the other maligned poverty types, who got discount lunches and food stamp care packages, who wore the same shirts and jacket year after year, who was called "Nature Boy" by my second grade teacher because my jacket was so thin, a spring coat in two feet of snow, and the other kids would laugh at me because she laughed at me too. Pin him in a corner and pile it on. Easy prey. Everywhere. All I knew was that there was one way out, and that was straight through. You had to keep going. You had to keep reading, writing, imagining a better place ahead, imagining a better place now. Years later, even with the bills and the medical debt and the failed love and the cars that die for no reason, you have to keep at it. The world will laugh at you, but if you keep your steel, you will find your moments. You will find your people and your chances. You will make it through. Because no matter how bad it gets, you can never forget —we're all terminal, but you still have a shot of making this hell something beautiful, if only for you, just you. Keep your head up, and let their laughter roll off like rain.

Native Songs

It is all around us, this end. How can the greatest fire of hope survive the reign of endless broken hearts falling from the midnight clouds, rushing, going? How can we rejoice in such lonesome weather? We must; it is the truth, even if the choirs deny our native songs—joy lives, if only to die, some day, far away.

You'll Go Blind

Three boys pawing through a green dumpster. Heaps of refuse and gladiator dreams of finding another magazine like the one Bennie found that afternoon—a Playboy magazine, February 1993 with a blood red cover and the model's legs so cigarette thin and spread like scissors, cutting apart our dumb youth and our unknowing, flagrant pre-teen idiocy. Astride the green metallic edge of the dumpster, I reached down and felt the pages, pulled, and a symphonic lustfulness percolated through my body, eyes stunned by this masculine brand of feminine overkill. We dove down for more, at least sixteen found altogether. Bennie and Gary and I ran down to the grove of pines behind the metallic bank of mailboxes and divvied them up. In the end I kept two and gave all my others to Bennie for the February '93, cigarette legs and all. I couldn't hardly open Feb. '93, I just stared at the cover in the flashlight darkness of my midnight room. The girls at school seem so far away now. But soon enough the girls at school began to catch up and things once missing suddenly flooded our eyes and minds, our basest idiocies flourishing, and the magazines were slowly forgotten with time, slipped away, gone to somewhere, but even now, the memories remain—the bright yellow sunshine glinting off the side of that beat and dusty dumpster, our stupid insistent search, the glory of our sin, and we never did go blind like people warned, although it's getting harder to see those old days, straining now with eyes like staring at the sun.

Are You Experienced?

We spoke of sex incessantly, while walking through the woods, while walking through the alleyways behind trailers and sheds. We spoke of sex while sitting on couches and on front stoops listening to Jimi Hendrix or Nirvana or playing Nintendo. And as always, we knew nothing. Jay was a few years older and his eighth grade class had just gone through sex ed, so he would recite his lessons to us, all very technical and illogical. What rubbish, yet what did we know? It was all a great mystery to us. Each of Jay's revelations only made us more curious, but then one day Bennie had enough, and Rick went with him. They were tired of the clinical sex talk and the ethical questions and all the wondering about what women are made of, and eventually the rest of us drifted away from all that talking too. Not from sex, especially not after we found those Playboys in Mr. Muller's trash bin, but those formal almost Plato-istic discussions of what and how and why. Looking back I suppose we no longer needed those because we'd find out soon enough. We'd experience that first stabbing pain of new love, and later the jarring awareness that haunts all of us before, during, and after sex, and how that awareness fades again to a series of heartbeats beating us senseless with muddled expressions of love, be they tame or angry, be they aware or lost, be they right or wrong, all of it pain, lust, and death, death, death, and more.

JITTERBUG

I lost fifteen fishing lures in a row out on Snyder's Pond before I decided I didn't know how to fish. Don't tell my step-dad. I owe him all that and more.

CROWS AND NIGHT BIRDS

Crows and night birds blanket the trees at dusk, line of somnolent pines and willows and maples jagged against fading purple horizon of farm and pine barren, the dusty yellow hues melting to nothing at all. Crows and night birds squatting to pray along the limbs and telephone wires. Crows and night birds taking off in the moving wind like a tornado of ash from our burning world. Youth shedding its dead muddied skin. Crows and night birds crying to each other in languages we will never know, hated by we for we cannot fly, we who will not know the joys of melting into the night sky, we who do not know much joy at all, and night birds know so much. As children we are caught between all the horrors of Man and all the prayers of crows and night birds, yet we remain lost, lost, lost to the prayers of their gods and ours, sun falling, gone to that next dark place.

Apocalypse Soon

Humanity is an endangered species on the cusp of a dull and sudden end; flashfire silence and one last look at some stranger's face that you never wanted to see in the moment you died, intense loneliness for one heartbeat moment, won't even hurt. Or maybe you will close your eyes in that precursor void and remember the cold exhalations curling up from your dog's nose in December when you were nine, sitting in the yard with him, his head on your legs, Polaris and the Big Dipper glinting in the frigid atmosphere above your trailer park home. Will that be enough for you before resounding nothingness eternal and pure? Don't worry, that moment hasn't come yet. Check your pocket. There's a ticket there. It says 8:30 pm, a bus that will arrive somewhere beyond the horizon, if it gets there at all. Those with you will depart as strangers, walking skeletons that will not curl up beside one another in the riptide death falling from above, reaching from below, some presidential mistake, some authoritarian revenge. Our world is dying but we're not dead yet. You live on. Your memories live on. Your pain and joy continue. Look out from the bus window down at people in their cars talking, singing, drinking coffee, ignoring the universe, ignoring the infinitesimal amount of time we have left. Watch the landscape roll by, landscape that will always be there, always silent, always, a human's sense of always, such a small paper cut of time. That moment under Polaris with a beagle in your lap may have happened seconds ago, may be happening now, decades later, infinite overlap, and with no traffic this bus will reach Albany, Burlington, Calhoun, Birmingham, Manhattan, Fresno, anywhere, any time, in no time. The universe has already forgotten you and you're right on time. It's all happening. It's all over. Go forth, oh passenger of snowflake awakenings, go find your child self and walk into the void together, falling, flailing, beautiful, melting, into that final void, apocalypse soon beneath beautiful Polaris.

BONES

Every time the doctor mentions the bone tumors from the CT/PET scans, I think of how afraid I was to ride my bike down the ravine and off the jump we set up. I was afraid to break my arm like Tony Scarpetti did the summer before. The silly things we once feared. I'm glad I jumped that ramp.

The Best Laid Plans of Mice and Men

My grandfather's typewriter sat on my desk among scattered Lego men and reams of lined paper, and at the age of twelve I decided it was high time to become my own publisher of comics, but how to create images on a typewriter? I spent days and weeks at home in my 7 x 8 room drawing stick figure superheroes, but now that I had the machine of professionals I had no idea how to translate my frantic, untamed visions into books, so I let the metal hulk sit and wait as I ran out of pens and paper, asking Mom for more, and I ran those dry as well. The stick-men soon grew dull. I needed something more. It was late summer, cusp of autumn, at the town-wide garage sale in Castleton where I went walking with Gary and Jess and I saw that table full of worn-down library books for a dime each; boxful for a buck. I had heard of the title before, *Of Mice and Men*, and I decided it would look good of me to carry around a scholarly-looking book, falsely thinking then (and for too many years after) that girls like a guy with bookish intelligence and creative fortitude. I'd carry it to school, see what people thought of me then. I took Mr. Steinbeck home and read his book in bed, a few pages a night before falling asleep. But each night found me pushing deeper into the book, a few pages more, just a few more, and in the final moments the gunshot that caught me in the heart. That shot rang all night long, and I wept into my pillow and stayed inside all the next day. My little superheroes now felt useless and tame. All their powers and costumes just dust in my mind. I brought the boxes of homemade comics to the dumpster down the street and let go of all those scribbles and fantasies. My grandfather's typewriter sat on my desk among scattered Lego men and reams of lined paper. At the age of thirteen, I decided it was time to discover what this shaking inside of my chest was supposed to mean. So I inserted a page, and I began.

WAKE UP TIME

Tom Petty on cassette through the dead brush and corn stalks gold and stunted in October. Crawling back to you. Don't fade on me. I'll never know the goodness of being king, but I'll know October in the setting sun. The world is a lonely place when you're alive, yet you're alive, with such higher places to go.

The Scary Parts

Six months down the line only to find the chemo didn't work, and the doctor begins to map out the next six months but all you heard were the words "tumor spread to your bones" and the way the sunlight glinting through the tenth story window just off 53rd Street cuts dazzling yellow shapes across the wall, reminding you of the way it did in autumn afternoons on bus rides home, when the sun would set earlier and earlier, the leaves red then gold then brown then gone, and you'd walk that half mile home from the bus stop through the trailer park, your sister lagging behind a little with her friends, but all you wanted was to get home and pull your comforter off your bed, sit on top of the heating grate, and create a cocoon of hot air radiating upward, a book in hand, the smell of dinner almost ready wafting down the long trailer hallway. It's the only place you wanted to be on a chilly November afternoon turning into evening, where if you were good and if it was a Friday night your mother would make you homemade chocolate milkshakes with popcorn straight from the big plastic popping machine with the wrrrrrrr-ing hot air, and she'd let you and your sister and her friends watch Gremlins on VHS just so long as you didn't get too scared but you never got too scared, did you? The scary parts would come later, much later, and when they did come you'd bury your hands in your face and sob alone in a studio in Queens and wonder how much a train ticket would cost to go north, not say a word, kiss your mother hello, curl up with a book, call your sister, and ask if she can remember when, the good and the bad, ask her to tell you all about it, see if her path back through the pines aligns with yours. It won't. It never does. But it helps you some, and you soon understand the only way is forward, full of scary parts, but maybe something more, just so long as you keep going, eyes peeking through your fingers covering your face all the way to the end.

Phantom

You could hear the TV through the trailer's thin walls at night as voices spoke of war and planes dropping bombs on men and oil, of places we'd never heard of like Kuwait and Baghdad and how far away was all this? Would those planes come here, to Pine Peaks Trailer Park? To Green Meadow Elementary? Would the hallway shadows shift with such malice if someone would just quiet that TV for a little while? Ghosts of planes and bombs skitter across the walls with each passing car outside the window, each a phantom bearing closer with its own religion of death, just for you there in your bunk bead, top bunk empty, brother in your parent's room, leaving you alone with the phantom, the voices, and eventually the dreams of burning oil spilling black plumes into the future of every 90s child, a horror you had no idea would get worse, and worse, and worse.

Ghost Train

I was twenty-four and it was late March when I pulled up in front of the long hothouse at the edge of the farm, feeling embarrassed and drained of any sense of pride I once had. The ground, like the sky, was cold, hard, wet, and filthy. It was wet inside too, hot and humid, an amazing 50 plus degree change. "Are you here for the job, the one to pick tomatoes?" she asked me. I said I was there to find out about it, that I'd read about it in the paper. I was really there for the money, a mere $6 an hour, but my marriage was wavering and I knew money sure as shit played a big role in its corrosion. I didn't know who I was or why I was or how growing up in poverty somehow marked me in a way you could only see once you lived with me for a year or so. I couldn't hold on to anything, not a job, not love. I knew the extra dough would be a stopgap. I hoped it would. The hothouse was raw with green chlorophyll and smelled thick with bruised stems and leaves. Young immigrant couples carried baskets and stoic faces. Their stained clothes hung cockeyed. I will look like that soon enough, I thought. I am fine with looking like anything that works. Anything to make it through. I made small talk and my heart sank because I knew she knew I couldn't do it as well as all these people here, working hard and fast. She maybe saw some welling conflict in me, some sorrow. I don't know. I took home an application anyway. On my way back, just past Salem, almost home, I pulled over and stared into a freshly tilled field and the stone farm house beyond. A plastic play set stood in the back yard with a tricycle sidewalks in the grass. I thought of Elliott Road and my youth, of my sister, of the feeling of closing your eyes when your bike was going so fast, the future dark and wide, welcoming. I remembered what hope felt like when it wasn't stained around the edges. I remembered summer break happiness and the smell of my grandfather's pool, cut grass and the grill fired up. I remembered the ignorance of youthful peace on a swing-set flying high. I opened my eyes and it all fell away. I saw there were railroad tracks beyond that stone farm house up by the distant tree line and I wanted a train to come by so bad, come and take me away, but it never did.

Dark Tunnel of Pine

Always the train station at night, age after endless age the gravel glows yellow between the tracks from lamppost lights in Hudson, in Beacon, in Cold Springs, and endless northward toward old home. Down the dark tunnel of pine where the tracks disappear the 10:20 local calls out like a wailing mother in search of her children. We rise from the benches, the few of us scattered up and down the platform, our shadows stretching out across the tracks, the rumble getting closer. Even with the anticipation, the heavy sensation of slumber begins to take hold, the journey back in time not over but perhaps now there will be a few hours just for us, when we don't have to feel the holes in the bottoms of our shoes or the knifing shards of cancer gutting us with each step down the sidewalk, road, life. This is the good part, the boarding, the feeling that we'll be safe here if only for a little while. A feeling we lost somehow. So we take these rails, these roads, these endless footpaths through the dark wood back to try and find it, even just a breadcrumb or two to show the way.

Maladies & Memories

The people in the big yellow trailer with the brick driveway, they gave out the best candy bars on Halloween. King-sized bars, and often toys too, a yo-yo or a paddle ball or stuffed animals in little Halloween costumes. All of us food stamp kids living in the trailer park would rush across yards of dogs, junked cars, rusted swing sets, past lit-up doorways filled with jack-o-lanterns and streaming white cobwebs, through crowds and karma in order to reach that one house. We had to get there before the gangs of kids from other neighborhoods came and took our candy. Some years we were lucky. Some years we were too late. All years we sang our song door to door as those grinning sawtooth jack-o-lanterns stared at us, cackling their fire, orange guts weeping fierce maladies and memories, howling at the darkness, too soon fading to black as the night came to an end for us all. That's how it was for many years, until someone started a fire behind the yellow trailer where the people who would hand out full candy bars lived. The police called it arson, started the day before Halloween, started by someone who didn't know they were taking away our magic, ripping the sleeve from our childhood, gouging the eyes of the jack-o-lantern souls flicking inside every one of us, which would also go out eventually. But maybe not for all of us. Some would hold on. I tried to hold on. Maybe I did, in a way, by remembering, a little light left somewhere in the catacombs beneath my adulthood. That night, that last true Halloween, there would be no flicker that night, no fire. Nothing but pulp and forever after we'd find tedious doorsteps of Novembers and decades of doldrums, lives beyond childhood, all of us Halloween survivors staring up at a half moon lilting through one stale night after another. Too young to catch that last Halloween magic, and now too old to go home again.

HUDSON

If you hound the river to its roots, you will find the awe of standing on stones and letting cool water trickle over your feet, reddish water hued by clay and copper, the sun powering down through the storm of black flies filling the air like pepper shook from the trees above, the air thick with June's humidity. The river begins so earnest and lithe, growing strong and wide long before trains run along its bank, trains leading to deathtraps and factories and car wrecks and children born and jazz-fueled mad-nights and love and hate and love again and bundles of cancerous masses folded into every blink of the eye, eyes that cannot see the water of the Hudson for what it is: the running depths of yesteryear, sweet silver bliss dappled by sun and shivering from the ocean's pull felt in New York harbor, Poughkeepsie shores, the locks in Troy and Waterford, all the way up to the smallest drops on the topmost pine trees singing from Adirondack peaks where it all begins. And everywhere in between, small nests of childhood memories, Hudson River daydreams and farms full of fumbling grasshoppers and rabbits, clusters of trailer park homes numbered one through eighty-three, one for you and one for me. But no matter how many times I try to go back there, it is a place of never-again, for water only runs one way until it ends at the sea, one beginning and one finale in this rushing torrent of life.

My Gratitude

We sometimes laughed at our mother when she tried to discipline us. She was so slight and small and it didn't hurt and we didn't want to be mean to her but we also couldn't stop the smiles, the grinning when she'd smack our shoulders, scold and demand, her fury genuine, her reasons true. But that one time I called her a hateful name and saw the sting, I wept. And that one time I broke her favorite glass dish and waited in the darkened living room for her to come home, I wept. And that one time years after we left the trailer park, just after graduating high school, when she cried and told me she wished she had been a better mother, I wept too. We were not the easiest millstones to carry, and those years in the trailer park were fraught with unemployment or three jobs at once, food stamps, sick children, fighting children, divorce, spoiled water, the fear of making wrong choices, of being trapped, of never getting out. Mom, we got out, and all the hells that came after weren't anyone's fault, least of all yours. In the rising tide and the falling skies, you were our utopia everything, the fire we'll carry through the night until there's nowhere else to go.

HIDING

I don't know why we talk so much and say so little, or mean so much and talk so little, or hurt so much and mean so little. But here we are, here I am in the dark of night with a window to the sidewalk and spilled wine on my sleeve, with memories of moving pianos during summer jobs, the scent of red hair held by ribbons, brilliant sunshine through maple trees dropping diamonds into the shade where we played as children behind our trailer and ate the raspberries we plucked from bushes all through the forest, all along the creek over by the abandoned summer camp. We're older now, hiding inside our homes and jobs and rooms and failing relationships not talking to each other as our bodies break down, in ways we see and in ways we don't. All I want is for us to make sure we don't regret the passing years, and hold on to a little of the sunshine coming down through the trees of our youth; stains on our fingers, love in our hearts.

ONLY IN DREAMS

Autumn with Weezer's Blue Album, my first purchase, driving riverside streets to Castleton, to the town-wide garage sale, cider donuts and laughter, ghost stories and the wind through the car window. At the Exxon station I'll ask Richie's mom for a Dr. Pepper, and then we'll keep driving into the night, looking for home. We'll never really find it, but that's okay with me.

One More Kiss 'Fore I Go

Every other road but the way out led to a hillbilly cul-de-sac and a shameful, incurable existence. Fifteen and friendly, Gary and Jess next door had moved months ago, and Barrett was long gone, Bennie's trailer burned down, and all I had left were jailbirds, gap-toothed ruffians, and a pack of nameless, faceless kids half my age who hid behind windows, never playing outside anymore, a vast kid-less ghost town. Bridges weren't just burned, it's almost as if they never existed. They have been dismantled, taken away in the night. Now with my braces and glasses and too-long gangly limbs, there was no chance of making it through this new landscape unless we got out, and so we got out, although not just for my sake—we had all had enough of Pine Peaks Trailer Park. The dreams had dried up, washed out, had become faded and moth-ridden. Even Halloween, Christmas, and one hundred Thanksgivings couldn't stop the feeling of heartbeat suffocation, the spiritual insomnia, the specter of a nothing future of pervasion, poisoned love, cancer wards, and maybe prison, which is where at least three former Peaks kids ended up after we loaded our truck and shipped out in the winter of '95, leaving behind only ghosts and gravestones marking half a childhood. There wasn't any regret, because that park had nothing else to give, and we took more than it originally had to offer. I still recall the one day I drove back there alone, over a decade later, divorced and disquieted, but educated by so many fresh highways full of trial and error, of books and exits, of love and loss. I was just then starting to see with the eyes I needed to make it through this life, jigsaw pieces coming together, and it was still long before the doctors gave me that news, their hands on my shoulder, telling me how the future would unfold. No, back then I was still sprawling and trekking and drinking up the nights and I drove all the way up to lot #78 and put it in idle, letting some Ryan Adams ease out of my stereo as I took in my old neighborhood in the fading afternoon sunlight. I saw the wood barrel flower-holders were still in front of the trailer, and the trees were twice as big and ten times as beautiful and lush, and the basketball court was still up. But the bike jump over near the ravine was overgrown, a dozen new trailers lined the streets, and the ghosts we left behind were long gone, the gravestones gone, the friends and laughter and uncontrollable tears gone. There wasn't anything else to remember. I turned my car around in the driveway where I once played with Matchbox cars and headed out of Pine Peaks Trailer Park for that last exit, feeling better for leaving, but saved for having been there in the first place.

About the Author

James H Duncan is the editor of *Hobo Camp Review*, a former editor with *Writer's Digest*, and is the author of such poetry collections as *Dead City Jazz*, *Dealing With the Devil in the Middle of the Road*, *Maybe a Bird Will Sing*, and *Berlin*, among others, and he has written two short story collections, *The Cards We Keep* and *What Lies In Wait*. After years on the road in bookshops, quiet pubs, chaotic diners, and on train station platforms looking for the next comfortable place to rest his head, he currently resides in upstate New York.

Somewhere inside of him is a twelve-year-old kid reading books in bed long after lights-out, sure to be tired for school the next day.

For more, visit www.jameshduncan.com.

Other Books by James H Duncan

Poetry
Dead City Jazz
Berlin
The Darkest Bomb (Lantern Lit, Vol. 1)
Dealing With the Devil in the Middle of the Road
Desolation 2 A.M.
Maybe a Bird Will Sing
Thrift Store Majestic
Welcome to the Night Shift

Fiction
What Lies In Wait
The Cards We Keep

www.ingramcontent.com/pod-product-compliance
Lightning Source LLC
Chambersburg PA
CBHW061336040426
42444CB00011B/2954